"To strip down, to purify, to breathe again, to remove the scum and the gilding has been a constant theme of Judaeo-Christianity, and so of the Western tradition. Look at the 'empty' churches of Sanraedam, the buildings of the Shakers, the piano music of Satie, or Cézanne's final watercolours… Emptiness in architecture – or empty space – is not empty, but full: yet to realize this fullness requires the most exacting standards."

Bruce Chatwin

Kodak
PROFESSIONAL FILM
5-EPY 135-36

LONDON
MINIMUM

HERBERT
YPMA

STEWART, TABORI & CHANG
NEW YORK

PAGES 2–3

A fanlight over the doorway to a London 'terrace' house illustrates the decorative influence of architect Robert Adam in the late 1700s. Amidst the classical revival of Georgian times, Adam established an entire design vocabulary based on the decorative detail of Etruscan architecture.

PAGES 4–5

In the minimal apartment of artists Adam and Carolyn Barker-Mills, architect Claudio Silvestrin designed an environment free from 'visual distraction'. Even the bookcases are shut behind doors that, when closed, blend with the walls.

PAGES 6–7

Cast iron picket fences are a distinct signature of inner-city London. The particular decorative forms of these spears, which vary from 'thistles' to 'fleur-de-lys', are stylized versions of 'classical influences'.

PAGE 8

London architecture is distinguished by a return to 'classicism'. Design in Georgian times looked to the Greeks and Romans and especially to the softer lines and studiously considered proportions of Palladio. Columns, pediments and architraves, reduced in scale and simplified, were used to decorate the building exteriors.

PAGE 12

Fashioned from two blocks of white Carrara marble, this sculptural hand basin, designed by John Pawson and Claudio Silvestrin, has become an icon for the new minimalism emanating from London.

PAGE 14

The manhole cover is a potent symbol of the changes brought to society by the Industrial Revolution. With the increased pace of life, modern necessities such as power, sewerage and drainage all had to be organized, preferably out of view. The 'utilities' would issue their own 'manhole cover', cast in the graphic style of the company.

To my parents, Carla and Peter, who have given me a more interesting and adventurous life than anyone could possibly hope for.

First published in Great Britain in 1996 by Thames and Hudson Ltd, London

Published in 1996 and distributed in the U.S. by
Stewart, Tabori & Chang,
a division of U.S. Media Holdings, Inc.
575 Broadway, New York, NY 10012

Distributed in Canada by General Publishing Co. Ltd.,
30 Lesmill Road, Don Mills, Ontario, Canada M3B 2T6

Library of Congress Catalog Card Number 95-72933
ISBN: 1-55670-478-X

Printed in Singapore
10 9 8 7 6 5 4 3 2 1

CONTENTS

INTRODUCTION

The 1980s is seen as the decade in which minimalism arrived in London. Shops such as Joseph, Equipment, Kenzo, Issey Miyake and Comme des Garçons used empty space as their new design statement and the work of architects Eva Jiricna, Armstrong and Chipperfield, Stanton and Williams and Pawson and Silvestrin commanded more than its share of glossy press. London became the world's hotspot for architecture and interiors that embodied the adage 'less is more'. Yet, despite all the publicity, London's minimal style was more often than not presented as a strange, temporary phenomenon. It was, after all, not very British!

Not much has changed. London's designers and architects are still producing the most sophisticated simplicity in the world and the press is still treating each project as a bit of a freak show. If journalists, however, did their homework, they would discover that a minimal approach is much more a part of the national character than they imagine. Like it or not, Britain has a strong 'reductivist' tradition.

From the restraint of Georgian London's classicism to the high-technology standardization of the Industrial Revolution, London's design history has always, in the words of Ralph Waldo Emerson, been a reflection of the nation's 'passion for utility'. It was a passion that Britain took into the 20th century in the work of George Gilbert Scott and the poetic reinforced concrete buildings of Tecton, through the Festival of Britain in the 1950s, and on into the 1960s, when London again scooped the world with Terence Conran's Habitat, the first chain of shops to bring the principles of 'good design' to the public; and then Mary Quant invented the miniskirt…

Over the past three or four centuries London has produced a staggering list of firsts in the world of architecture and design. All have been part of a desire to 'cut to the quick'. What, after all, could be more British than that?

1

INTERIORS

We are a curious race. We value our privacy, yet given half a chance we are more than prepared to take a good look around our neighbour's house. How people live creates in us an almost intuitive and insatiable curiosity.

Modern Alarms
Resident permit holders only
P

CLASSIC

CUTTING EDGE

When Sir Christopher Wren designed the Royal Hospital at Chelsea to house army veterans in the late 17th century, his ambitions included a grand plan to link the hospital and Kensington Palace with an impressive tree-lined boulevard. Sadly, all that was ever built of his master plan is a narrow tree-lined square dating back to 1692, now known as Royal Avenue.

It was on this historic site almost three hundred years later that Richard Rogers, one of London's most famous international architects, decided to convert a pair of adjacent classical terrace houses into a home for himself and his family.

The original stucco exterior of the 1840s gentleman's houses gives nothing away about the radical interior, unless of course one happens to be walking by at night when the curtainless windows of the *piano nobile* reveal an impressive open loft-like space. Where there were originally eight rooms, Rogers has created just one. He likes to joke that whereas most people turn barns into houses, he has turned his houses into a barn. But the space is really more like a piazza than a barn: a place of activity and interaction, where all sitting, cooking and eating take place.

What is fascinating about the interior of this house is how Rogers has been able to incorporate almost all of the signature features and details that distinguish his public buildings such as Lloyds of London or the Centre Pompidou in Paris: there is the creation of the impressive public space (in this case the 'white cube piazza'); the open transition from space to space; and the bold use of utilities and services as an undisguised partner in the overall design theme. Free-standing vertical ducts clad in textured stainless steel house the cables and pipes supplying electricity, water, heating and fresh air, further enhancing the feeling of space and height. Even Rogers's preference for 'raw' industrial materials blends unexpectedly well within this 'classical' container. The transparent metal stairs are micro-engineered pieces of high technology, yet their lightness of construction feels perfectly at home in the airy main space. Similarly, the tall, slender kitchen storage cabinets cased in stainless steel

sheeting convey more the feeling of a kitchen of serious culinary pursuits than a concern for industry. Rogers has also managed to introduce his trademark blue in the form of a bright steel beam dissecting the white space and his signature yellow comes back in the massive custom-designed lacquered bed.

Now, six years after initial completion, the children have grown up and moved out of the house. That's why early in 1995 the scaffolding went up and a complete redesign of the interior took place. Rogers wanted the mezzanine floor, which was previously used as the bedroom, for his study. The new bedroom would then take up the third floor, formerly the children's domain, but there was a problem: all the dividing walls had been taken out and the ceilings were, by comparison, rather low. So it was decided to break through one end and open this floor up to the central space too. What was once a grand double-height space has now become an even grander space with a triple-height 'well' under a freshly constructed transparent section in the roof (it's too large even to consider calling it a skylight).

This has brought even more light into what is now a towering space and has afforded the opportunity to add another transparent steel staircase, identical to the one leading to the mezzanine, rising in the opposite direction to the new bedroom.

More light, more privacy and more space are the rewards for undertaking the latest series of bold interior reconfigurations. It is difficult to imagine a better and more inspiring contemporary use of the faultless geometry of classical architecture.

PREVIOUS PAGE (16)
The exterior of this elegant 1840s late Georgian terrace provides only a tantalizing hint of the radical interior. The curtainless windows reveal glimpses of the towering three-storey open plan space: a vast white cube in a Georgian box.

PREVIOUS PAGES (18–19)
Viewed from above, the living area, with its massive expanse of uncluttered space, its profusion of natural light and white-painted floor, gives the Series 7 chairs designed by Arne Jacobsen and the Nomos table a jewel-like intensity.

OPPOSITE PAGE
The original steel staircase and its recently added 'mirror image' provide a good sense of the immense scale of the main space. The intervention of walls has been kept to a minimum. In keeping with the powerful poetry of so much unencumbered space, personal impedimenta have been kept to a bare minimum.

FOLLOWING PAGES (22–23)
An impressive double-height space has recently been converted into an even more dramatic triple-height space. The mezzanine floor, previously used as the bedroom, has now become the study, and a second staircase leads to the new third-floor bedroom gallery.

FOLLOWING PAGES (24–25)
The new bedroom on the third floor is dominated by a piece of mini-architecture. Designed and produced by Abe Rogers as a single, seamless, monolithic block of matt lacquer in Richard Rogers's signature yellow, its simple, symmetrical front façade hides a 'metropolis' of storage drawers on the rear-facing side of the block.

THE RIVER CAFE COOK BOOK

1	2	3	4
5	6	7	8

PHOTOS IN ORDER OF APPEARANCE – PREVIOUS PAGES (26–27)

1

A view through the mezzanine bathroom reveals the masonry detail referred to most commonly as 'quoin', distinctive dressed stonework on the corners of buildings.

2

The 1995 reconfigurations of the internal space in the wake of the children's departure have seen the conversion of the mezzanine floor from bedroom into study. A second staircase leads to the new third-floor bedroom gallery.

3

The bathrooms are simple yet elegant, continuing a theme of careful detailing and well-chosen materials. Note the long slender stainless steel handle on the square pivoting window. Even the ceiling is covered in the ubiquitous white square tiles. The wall of mirrors against which the washbasin is mounted stops the space becoming claustrophobic.

4

The structural detailing of the stairs in the main space is indicative of Rogers's fascination with the technology of bracing, used extensively for the Centre Pompidou.

5

A recent internal reconstruction has extended the massive white atrium space to include the previously isolated third floor. This floor, now the master bedroom, is flooded with daylight from the newly created skylight and the landing of its stainless steel suspended staircase hangs dramatically over a void, sixty feet deep.

6

The treads of the two high-tech staircases are fashioned from sheets of perforated stainless steel. They provide an unusual sensation by flexing slightly when stepped on, which lends an aspect of 'dynamic tension' to the everyday use of the space.

7

Where once there was a single high-tech staircase, the addition of a second rising in the opposite direction has provided a balance to the way it intrudes into the area. The sheer verticality has magnified the impression of space.

8

In true modernist style the interior spaces are subjected to the rigorous discipline of mathematical symmetry: a feature demonstrated quite clearly by the placement of the bathroom window within the tiled wall. A square of window equals a number of square tiles.

OPPOSITE PAGE

With just more than enough room to walk behind the bed, the beautifully proportioned rectangular layers of storage, punctuated by small high-tech brass drawer pulls, provide an elegant solution to storage needs. The integrity of the bedroom space is preserved without sacrificing space in which to put things.

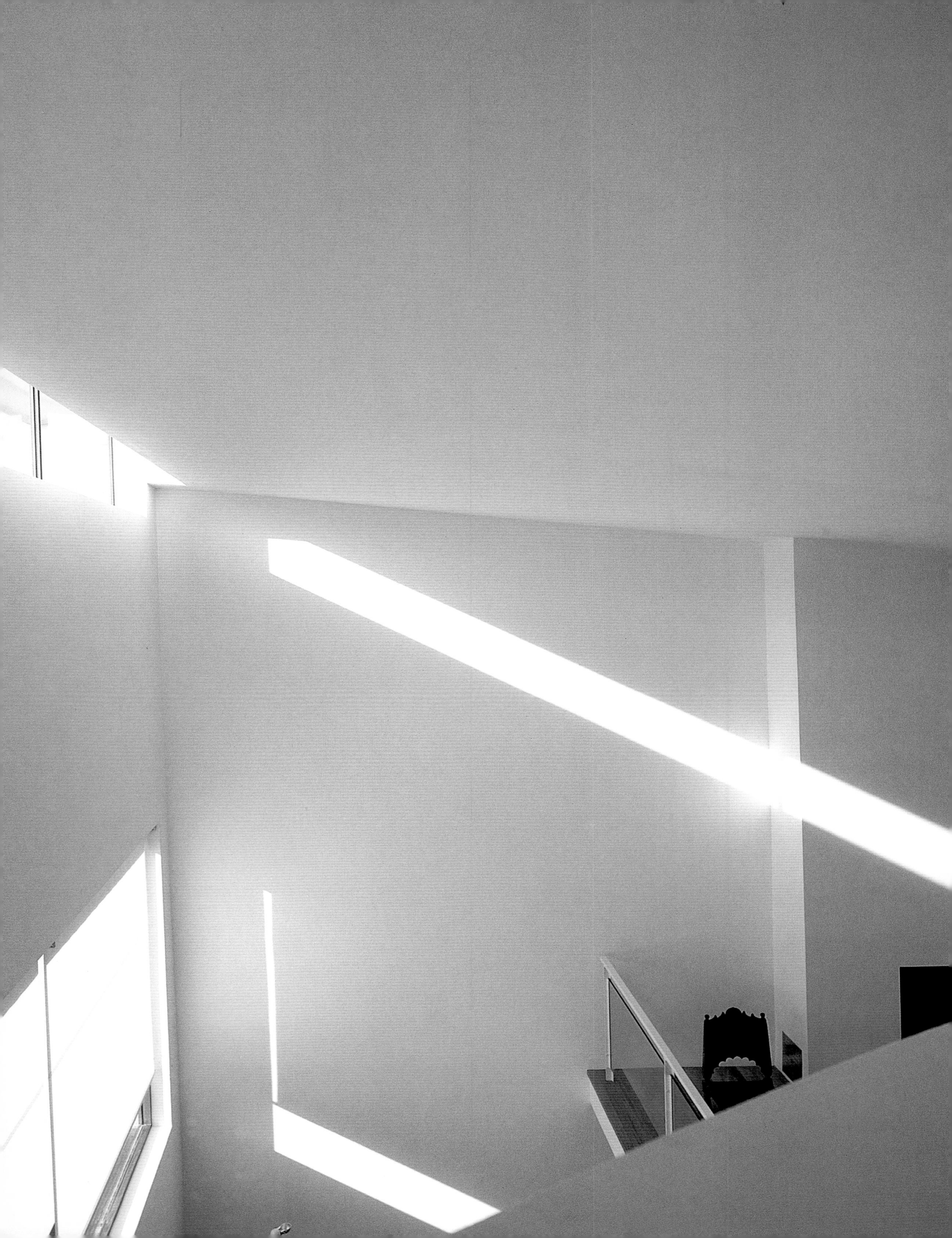

LIKE WHISTLER'S WHITE HOUSE

Upon seeing the house architect Pip Horne has recently designed for acclaimed minimalist Anish Kapoor, I was reminded of the story of James Abbott McNeill Whistler's house in Chelsea a hundred years earlier.

Whistler's White House was his dream.

Always immaculately turned out, Whistler's personal presentation was as carefully considered as the drawings and paintings over which he would labour constantly. His taste in house decoration was equally pronounced and years ahead of its time. His furniture was of the simplest. He sat on straight-backed chairs, used Japanese matting and abolished wallpaper, painting the walls in plain colours that he mixed himself.

It should come as no surprise, then, that Whistler at one point turned his hand to architecture. Together with E.W. Godwin, he embarked on something unique: a house that imitated no period and conformed to no existing fashion. The walls were of white-painted brick, the roof of green slate and, most extraordinary of all, the windows were placed where they were needed with no regard for symmetry. It was plain and radical, so plain that Whistler had to agree to paint a frieze on the outside of the building to placate local council concerns at its total lack of 'distinguishing detail'. Sadly, it was a dream he was never allowed to finish. Whistler went bankrupt in May 1879 and the house, together with its contents, went to auction. Had he been allowed to complete the house and live in it as he had imagined, with simple furniture set against monochrome walls, he might well have accelerated the modern movement in British architecture, such was his power and influence.

Back in the present, it was perhaps the asymmetrical placement of the windows that first struck a chord in my mind, but more than likely it was the fact that Pip Horne's design is, like Whistler's, plain and radical. It imitates no period and conforms only to the lifestyle of its inhabitants.

Unlike Whistler's experience, however, this project didn't end in disaster. Incredibly, it is the successful result of a property development scheme. On the site of a former furniture factory in a back lane of a 'hip' but not 'highbrow' end of

town, five architects developed five individual houses for five individual clients. A formula for disaster or an opportunity to break the mould? Certainly Pip Horne saw it as the latter.

The result is a sublime house, minimal in the truest sense because it relies purely on space and light for its success. It also happens to be Horne's first real project since graduating from the Royal College of Art in 1976. His previous projects have mainly involved extensions to houses; well executed but not exactly high-profile stuff. This doesn't seem to worry him. He is right when he says that architecture is 'an old man's game'. Van Day Truex, the legendary, long-serving design director of Tiffany's, only had one piece of advice for aspiring designers and architects: 'Wait as long as you absolutely, positively can before you build anything.'

Horne has waited a long time to do a building like this and it shows. Patience, restraint and maturity resonate throughout. It is a confident house, reflecting a client who knew what he wanted and an architect who was able to provide it. It is also a house of contrasts. Walls in finely finished plaster mix with ceilings and floors of bare concrete. Space, likewise, is either condensed or expanded by the architecture. To accommodate a third level, the ground-floor ceiling was lowered to stay within the overall height restriction; Horne balanced this compression with a towering atrium. One extreme sets off the other.

Throughout the house, careful consideration has also been given to daylight. Although not immediately noticeable, floors in the upper levels of the house finish short of the walls and the gap is filled with strips of laminated, toughened glass, creating a floor that allows daylight to filter along the walls into the building. On the other side of the house, the side that faces an internal courtyard, the mezzanine living area enjoys a sweeping view through a long rectangular expanse of glazing. By contrast, the ground floor is focused on a single square opening that provides a framed view of the garden. Although all five of the houses in the complex share this one garden courtyard, the strategic placement of windows and openings by Horne creates the impression that it is the domain of Kapoor's alone.

PREVIOUS PAGE (30)
The mezzanine of the atrium space is distinguished by carefully considered sources of daylight, an Indian prayer chair, a Rajasthani village table, an African stool and a stone icon.

PREVIOUS PAGES (32–33)
An important detail of the house is the square 'cut out' view of the courtyard. It creates the illusion that it is a private domain – when in fact the courtyard is shared with four other houses.

OPPOSITE PAGE
A view from the ground floor (which is a metre lower than ground level to allow the second storey to fit within the height restrictions) reveals the play between space, light and form.

THE CONVERSION OF CONVENTION

Mark Guard is hesitant to call himself a minimalist. He is concerned there is a danger that the attraction of minimal, white architecture can turn into a mere decorative 'trend', losing its initial and direct relationship to function.

Guard started his working life with architects such as Richard Rogers and Eva Jiricna, which can only have honed his minimalist instincts. However, he insists his work is not a process of reduction, but one of addition – adding layers of *function*. But what does that mean in real life? His conversion of a small terrace house in London's Soho perhaps best conveys his approach. Out of the collective floor space of three shoebox-size rooms he has created two independent apartments.

The secret lies in a dynamic conversion of the existing space. By literally pushing a button, a spring-loaded door, which looks more like a wall, sweeps across a space, bridging a gap between opposing walls, and *presto!* – a completely private bedroom, guestroom, study or whatever is desired is created. The push-button breaks the flow of electricity to a powerful electromagnet holding the pivoting wall/door in place, at which point a spring forces it to open out. The effect of a significant expanse of wall swooping automatically across an open space out of its recessed hideaway is James Bond at his best. The Soho house contains no fewer than four or five of these contraptions and one can imagine the havoc that would ensue if they did not fit exactly into their predetermined configurations.

Thus Mark Guard spends his clients' money on creating a choice of space. Within an urban context this would seem to be one of the most intelligent approaches of all. The opportunity to change the 'interior architecture' with the push of a discreet little button would have to rate as the ultimate in convenience and luxury.

A recent project in Paris is another example. In a single, beautiful, but small space, unified by a stone-tiled floor that runs out to include a balcony, high technology is put to work. Press a button and an entire slab of previously hidden wall swings out to enclose a private bedroom. Press another and an unexpected guest can be accommodated with privacy.

The bathroom, which appears precariously un-private behind a glass wall, enjoys a view through the entire space. Until, that is, one pushes yet another button. Instantly the clear glass becomes opaque, as if it had suddenly been sandblasted. How does it work? Rather like a polarizing filter. The glass is embedded with a high conductivity sheet that is in alignment to allow light to go through and goes out of alignment when charged with current.

All innovations raise questions and with Guard's work the main one seems to be: How does it relate to large spaces, where the call for versatility is not so pressing? A conversion of an old packing plant at New Concordia Wharf provides the answer.

At 3,000 square feet, a space that virtually hangs over the Thames is hardly a 'tight squeeze', yet Guard's ideas about transformation are just as applicable. The most obvious innovation is the railway tracks that run through the middle of the space. The explanation for them is, almost disappointingly, quite practical: the client didn't want to be restricted in his choice of location for the dining table, yet he could hardly drag a table suitable for six or eight around by himself.

Two tables set into the stainless steel tracks on spring-loaded roller bearings provide the solution. One table, a slab of green glass on slim, elegant stainless steel legs, is intended for eating, and the other, identical except for a more practical stainless steel surface, is designed to roll towards the 'dining' table loaded with goodies, rather like a supply wagon. A practical and decidedly poetic innovation.

All attempts at decoration have been put aside. It is a place that looks best bare. Perhaps a Brancusi or Moore (a small one) would not go amiss, but it does very well without. Almost as though he couldn't help himself, practicalities such as guest accommodation have been taken care of with Guard's signature 'swooping walls'.

Less is more … at the push of a button.

PREVIOUS PAGE (36)
The glass roof of a small terrace conversion in Soho is the largest self-supporting slab of domestic glass in London. It creates the impression of an outside room and provides an impressive view of the BT Tower.

OPPOSITE PAGE
A staircase in this previously derelict Grade Two listed building in Soho, completely converted by the architect Mark Guard, is constructed entirely of glass and delicately cantilevered out of the wall. It makes for quite a spellbinding effect – the stairwell is filled with light from a sash window above and the glass takes on different qualities as light moves across the glass treads during the day. The individual steps were laminated with perspex for strength.

1	2	3	4	5	6
7	8	9	10	11	12
13	14	15	16	17	18

PHOTOS IN ORDER OF APPEARANCE – PREVIOUS PAGES (40–41)

1

In a large converted warehouse plaster walls appear to float above limestone floors with the aid of a 'shadow gap'.

2

A North London two-storey Victorian terrace has been converted into a dramatic light-filled space.

3

The shower has an open view, unless privacy is required, in which case the 'privalite' glass becomes opaque at the touch of a button.

4 & 17

A Paris apartment reveals the versatility and value of 'privalite' glass: seen as opaque in photo 4 and clear in photo 17.

5

The rear of this North London terrace reveals a double-height space with a second staircase from the upstairs living area to the garden.

6

Viewed from below: this glass table, acting as a balustrade, is a clever means of following council regulations. The table would make it very difficult to fall over the edge.

7

The largest single sheet of self-supporting glass ever used in London domestic architecture illuminates a small kitchen.

8

A heated stone bath in Paris has a peephole window looking out of the back. The bath sits under a ceiling of glass.

9

An all-glass balustrade in a London terrace house maintains an uninterrupted view of the garden from the upstairs living area.

10, 15 & 18

The dynamics of a single space. In 10 the bedroom is open and the bathroom is closed. In 15 both bathroom and bedroom are open and in 18 both are closed.

11

Stairs that lead to a roof garden reveal Guard's respect for space. Hiding the stairs internally would have encroached on valuable living space.

12

A 7-metre-long steel counter travels across three different floor levels to create a coffee table at one end, a kitchen counter in the middle and breakfast table at the other end.

13

A cleverly conceived white steel frame supports a substantial sheet of horizontal glass that acts as high-tech canopy.

14

A shower is accommodated in the smallest and most efficient space possible for the task – namely a cylinder.

16

A floor-to-ceiling aluminium extrusion in a converted London terrace house is used as a very refined cover for the radiator.

OPPOSITE PAGE

The table, stainless steel with a green glass top, is set on roller bearings into a recessed stainless steel track to allow it to be moved around.

FOLLOWING PAGES (44–45)

From the stainless steel kitchen, tucked into a corner of this massive old warehouse on the Thames, the table on tracks has been designed to allow the client to change the venue for dinner or lunch without any effort at all.

BURNISHED BEAUTY

By all accounts, London is a welcoming metropolis for worldly types. On a Victorian street in Shepherd's Bush, the converted 'terrace' of Yvonne Sporre and Koji Tatsuno fits the bill as an example of London's complex crossover of influences and styles, a testament to the sophisticated success of culture-surfing.

Yvonne Sporre is Swedish-born but of Russian descent. She spent six years of her youth in Italy and much of her early adult life travelling around as a top international model. She doesn't see herself as Swedish or any other nationality for that matter. Her partner Koji Tatsuno was born in Japan but ended up in London as a fashion designer after a buyer for Browns asked him to run up a dozen shirts like the one he was wearing, cut from an old kimono. He is more comfortable in London. As he says: 'I grew up in Tokyo but it was the Tokyo of TV and computers. I like to be free and I don't like rules or labels.' Together they make quite a pair of cultural vagabonds. It was perhaps inevitable that they would end up in London.

The originality of their living space is, appropriately, a reflection of their tastes. The influences of various countries and cultures are pared down and remixed within the confines of an unadorned interior. An eccentric, eclectic collection of things creates a world of burnished beauty. Theirs is a completely different 'take' on minimalism. It has the focus on space and light and the discipline in terms of the reduction of clutter, but it is also romantic in an ethereal sort of way. Yvonne Sporre's original intention was for it to resemble the interior of an old Scandinavian castle: grand but spare, impressive but not pompous. 'Romantic' was certainly not part of her brief. Nonetheless, it is – in mood and atmosphere: the romance of faraway places, of travel and discovery, the mystery of the unknown.

In a broader discussion of minimalism this interior is significant. It demonstrates clearly that *reduction*, as a means of getting to the essence of a place, does not have to take away charm, beauty or character. The space may be unadorned but it is not bare. As Doris Saatchi, ardent supporter and patron of the minimal approach, says: 'A good space will accommodate an Empire chair every bit as well as a Corbusier chaise'... or a Rajasthani daybed, as the case may be.

The house started out as an earnest little Edwardian terrace. Sporre had the entire interior gutted. Walls were torn down, ceilings raised and almost all traces of the original plan removed, with the exception of the windows. The entire ground and

first floors were turned into large, single, light-filled spaces. This is not an approach for the timid. Once you knock out all the walls it is too late to change your mind. But Sporre knew exactly what she wanted and hired architect J.F. Delsalle, a friend from Paris, to do it. The radical structural changes have resulted in an astonishing sense of space and light. Even the pair of 19th-century Gothic stone fireplaces were set flush into the wall to allow the space to continue uninterrupted and the lime-bleached oak floors to run throughout. It forms an appropriate backdrop to Yvonne Sporre and Koji Tatsuno's odd collection of things.

An overgrown garden, a 19th-century jeweller's table, a teardrop church chandelier with the letter 'M' for Madonna engraved on each crystal leaf... These are the ingredients of a rarefied atmosphere, like that of an alchemist's lab. In the truest spirit of minimalism each object has to justify itself. These are not the haphazard choices of a compulsive consumer, but 'permitted intrusions' that have proved their worth.

Minimalism is not, as is commonly believed, a style that precludes possession, it is a style that precludes *careless* possession. As Doris Saatchi says: 'Such living demands discipline, planning and vigilance. Neatness, cleanliness and maintenance are paramount... It requires time and effort but it has its rewards: freedom from the tyranny of knick-knacks.'

PREVIOUS PAGE (46)
This Shepherd's Bush terrace stops at the door. Once inside, one enters a new dimension, a rarefied atmosphere of a fascinatingly diverse choice of pieces and influences. The common signature is a lack of convention and an individual sense of worth. Each piece, such as this asymmetrical 'wing chair' (with only one wing), has wit and presence.

PREVIOUS PAGES (48–49)
The main living area downstairs, a substantial gallery-like space, was created by removing partition walls and corridors and by eliminating all cornices, kick boards and gutters. To maintain the uninterrupted flow of the space the stone fireplaces were set flush into the walls. The cut-glass chandelier, the asymmetrical wing chair, the Rajasthani village table and the Fortuny studio lamps all point to a well-defined sense of style: clarity and confidence, the classic hallmarks of successful 'minimalism'.

OPPOSITE PAGE
The first floor, like the ground floor, has been totally remodelled by breaking away internal walls and extending the space vertically to within the confines of the roof. An eclectic collection of bits of furniture and objects is arranged as a soothingly sophisticated still life. Old apothecaries' wooden chests on bare boards, a silver Fortuny reflecting lamp, a mat of woven coconut husks and a wicker prayer chair are a reflection of an Oriental–Occidental mix that defies categorization.

FOLLOWING PAGES (52–53)
In these two photos, steps, fashioned from steel rods, lead from the first-floor bedroom up and through a submarine-like hatch into a tiny attic space intended for use as a spare bedroom. The round skylight illuminating the space mimics the circular hatch entrance to the space.

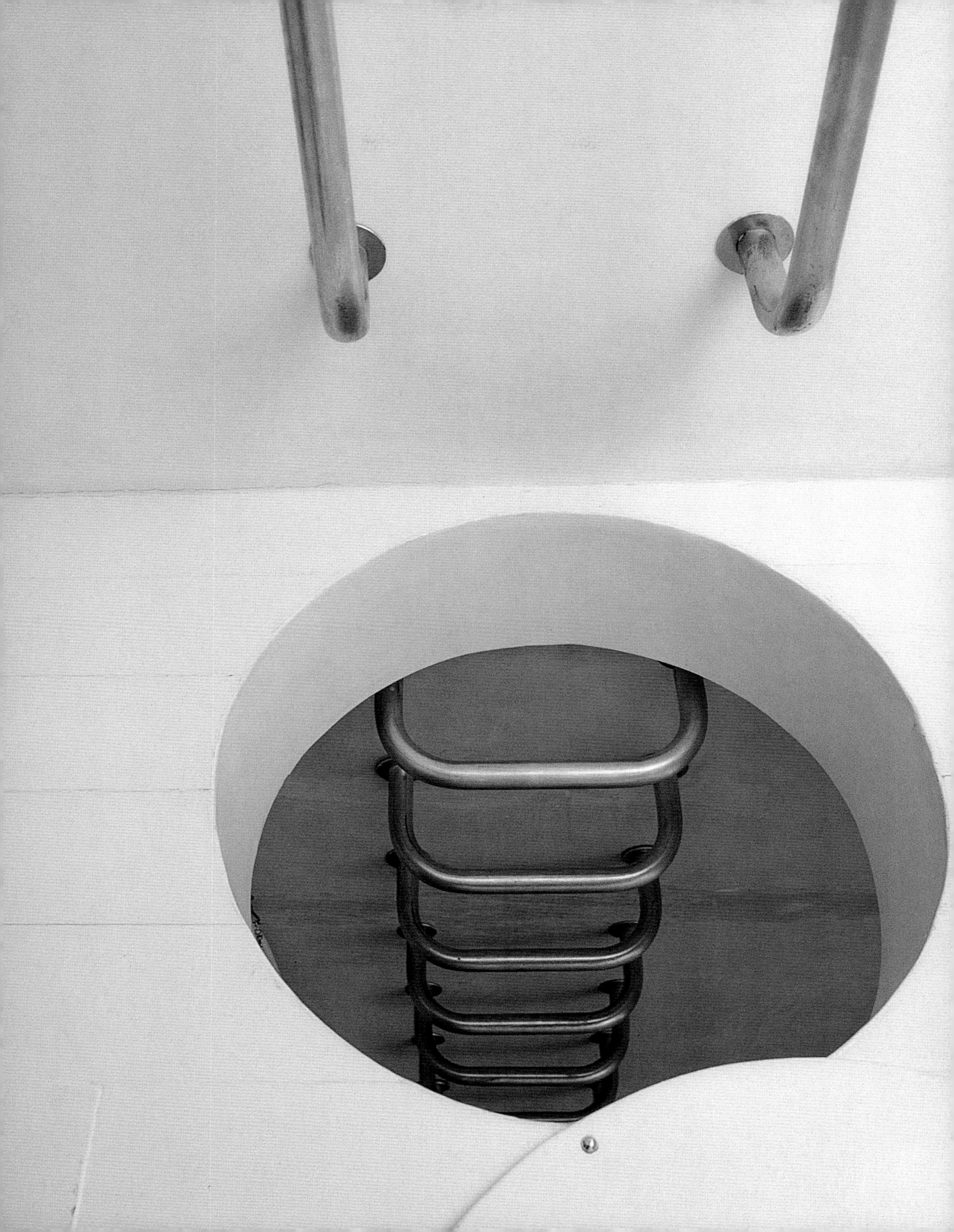

SOFT

SPARSE

SIMPLICITY

Seeking out more space is part of a long-standing London tradition. City-dwellers in search of larger spaces, cleaner air and less disease were responsible for the eventual development of Greater London. As early as the mid-1800s even shopkeepers and clerks started to seek out mansions in areas such as Peckham. What was at one time a series of sleepy villages was eventually swallowed up into an ever increasing and further sprawling metropolis.

It is a tradition that has continued unabated and it has led, in recent years, to the residential development of the Docklands. Once the hub of Britain's brisk trade with the 'Colonies', these vast riverside warehouses are now being converted into what can perhaps best be described as 'loft condominiums'. The primary attraction is space.

In its early years the port of London was nothing more than a succession of timber wharfs and a handful of shabby cellars and outbuildings.

It wasn't until midway through the 18th century that the exponential growth of commerce left an architectural residue worthy of mention. London was by then Britain's chief port and the colonial 'Empire' was doing good business, so good that chaos and disorder were caused by all the ships waiting to unload. In an effort to get a grip on the situation an Act of Parliament in 1799 enabled the City and some commercial partners to start building a much-needed dock on the Isle of Dogs. It was called the West India Dock. Then came the London Dock at Wapping, followed by the East India Dock at Blackwall and St Katharine Dock adjoining the Tower. As John Summerson comments in his definitive text *Georgian London*: 'All were promoted by private companies; all were planned broadly and well; and all availed themselves of the best ability in engineering, and produced architectural results which combined structural originality, unadorned, with a strong sense of the classical.' The promise of profit had fuelled a construction boom that resulted in structures that had, so to speak, 'good bones'.

It was these bones, admittedly threadbare and disused, that first attracted Sue Skeen to a floor of a former wine warehouse on the south bank of the Thames in Bermondsey. Sue Skeen made a name for herself in London with a pared-down

aesthetic that has been a force in both the magazine and the catalogue publishing world. Starting, as many have, under the critical but knowing eye of Min Hogg at the *World of Interiors*, she eventually went out on her own and has recently, amongst other things, coordinated the production of the Habitat catalogue. She has simplified Habitat's presentation, photographing many products in houses designed by architects renowned for their minimalism. This no doubt also crystallized her plans for her own space.

The place Skeen found for herself in London's Docklands area had all the qualities she was looking for: floor-to-ceiling loading bays, heavy steel industrial doors, a view framing Tower Bridge, good light and massive dimensions. Starting from scratch, Skeen chose to create a separate bedroom and bathroom and to leave the remaining space as a flexible living area. Furniture is grouped in clusters in different places for different functions. A pair of loose-covered armchairs by the loading-bay doors command the best view. Diverse chairs grouped around a solid maple workbench table of her own design indicate a place to work and also to eat and entertain. But none of the furniture or its function is taken too seriously. All the heavy stuff is on castors because the main message is 'mobility'. She relishes the idea of being able to move everything around and to her this flexibility is a key component of the luxury of space.

Although it is sparsely furnished, Skeen's warehouse has a warm and inviting quality. The secret lies in the quality of light that floods the interior and in the clever and consistent blend of gentle surfaces and patinas. Everything may be white and minimal but nothing is cold, hard or clinical. It is a white space that soothes and reassures the eye, and the few unpretentious things that furnish it are as casually arranged as seashells on a shore.

PREVIOUS PAGE (54)
The loading-bay doors of the former wine warehouse open out onto a view of the Thames, Tower Bridge and the dome of St Paul's beyond.

PREVIOUS PAGES (56–57)
Sue Skeen allowed the space to dictate how she should live. The white walls and vast expanse of solid maple floor accentuate the open expanse.

OPPOSITE PAGE
A solid maple table of her own design is set on castors. Everything can be – and is – moved around continually. Arrangements of white boxes and old books create vertical 'vistas'.

FOLLOWING PAGES (60–61)
A practical, pared-down aesthetic – in keeping with the building's utilitarian past – is expressed with a signature preference for vertical stacks in neutral hues.

FOLLOWING PAGES (62–63)
A pair of port and starboard 'blades' reflect her love of the river (she rows in a double scull) and a small wooden display cabinet filled with dismembered plaster extremities is an offbeat reminder that she does not take decoration all that seriously.

2

T. SAMPSON LTD
EUSTON ROAD N.W.

2

ORIGINS

None of us exists in a vacuum. Everything about us, where we live and how we live, is inextricably linked to how our forebears lived. Connected to our ancestors via distinct forms, patterns, rhythms and shapes, we belong to societies that are in a continuing balancing act between forging forward and looking back. We cannot escape history and tradition.

GEORGIAN LONDON

ELEGANCE

AND

RESTRAINT

In 1938 Robert Byron was invited by the BBC to participate in a scripted debate on the merits of preserving London's Georgian architectural heritage. His script was not printed at the time but was later included by John Summerson in the epilogue of his *Georgian London*. Byron's succinct text is, perhaps, the perfect introduction to the special relevance of Georgian architecture to London's history.

'Generally speaking it wasn't until the eighteenth century that the square and the streets we know today were designed to show off houses of a particular style and height. The Georgian style commemorates a great period, when English taste and English political ideas had suddenly become the admiration of Europe. And it corresponds with our national character. Its reserve and dislike of outward show, its reliance on virtue and dignity of proportions only and its rare bursts of exquisite detail, all express as no other style has done that indifference to self advertisement, that quiet self assumption of our worth, and that sudden vein of lyric affection which have given us our part in civilisation.'

It all started with the introduction of 'taste'. Inigo Jones, a gentleman of knowledge and distinction who had spent a few years in the heady atmosphere of Renaissance Italy, returned to London in the early 1600s eager to introduce the perfect proportions of Palladio to his native land and obtained permission to build London's first 'piazza' at Covent Garden. Although few knew what to make of it at first, his Palladio-inspired buildings laid the foundation stone of two centuries of London taste.

Palladianism eventually conquered not only the architecture of high places, the public and private buildings of government and wealthy patrons, but through books it also found its way to the workshop of the humble carpenter and bricklayer.

Inseparable from the popular taste for Palladio was the style's suitability for property development. The Earl of Bedford, in building the first so-called 'square' in Bloomsbury in around 1661, invented a particularly clever formula for generating wealth from property – a system that continues to this day. A parcel of freehold land would be divided into many identical strips surrounding a green square. Each narrow

lot would be granted a long lease (99 years). This is where the proportions of Palladio were so perfectly appropriate. The Georgian terrace house was, in simple terms, a stripped-down Palladian façade repeated all the way down the street. Builders, private speculators or any manner of ambitious journeymen would be encouraged to build a house on a plot at their own cost and then sell the house and lease to a 'bumpkin' looking to buy his first townhouse.

It was an ingenious system, for it held the key to being able to make property generate wealth over and over again. The landlords, eager to maintain the ability of these properties to create wealth for their heirs, were thus concerned to ensure a certain level of building quality. All of this was further promoted by the introduction of the great Building Act of 1774, a milestone in the history of London's architectural improvement. It provided a standard of order and dignity and laid down strict minimum standards for building. The Act also saw to it that the London house should not adorn itself with any but the most reticent kinds of ornament. Here was architectural minimalism enforced by law. What more convincing historical precedent for 'minimalism' could one possibly hope to find?

"A handful of aristocrats had their insulated palaces; and the unemployable and criminal classes had their centuries-old rookeries; but the remainder, from earls to artisans, had their narrow slice of building, now called, for no very good reason, 'terrace' houses."

John Summerson

GEORGIAN LONDON, 1991

PREVIOUS PAGE (66)
Robert Adam, one of the most widely celebrated of the 'Georgian classicists', was inspired by the pure, elegant lines of ancient Greek and Roman ruins. Thus, Etruscan urns and other figures would also eventually find their way onto and into London architecture.

PREVIOUS PAGES (68–69)
The oyster shell represents the appearance of the Rococo love of decorative whimsy on the otherwise restrained face of Georgian architecture and design. Throughout Georgian times this extravagant ornamental influence would surface in English decorative arts and architecture.

OPPOSITE PAGE
The fascination with the pineapple is most intriguing. Throughout the city it adorns stately pillars and gateways. Pineapples, very surprisingly, have been cultivated in Scotland since the early 18th century, and one explanation for their popularity in British design is that they are symbolic of mankind's triumph over nature and the elements – an image of an exotic tropical fruit flourishing in the chilly northern lands.

THE SEDUCTIVE PROMISE OF THE INDUSTRIAL REVOLUTION

Halfway through the 19th century, Britain experienced simultaneous exponential growth in population, prices, gross national product and wages. In economic terms this represented the Holy Grail, a modern miracle, a goal politicians would strive a lifetime to achieve and never pull off.

Towns and cities multiplied in number and size and a whole new urban society emerged. It was the dawning of the age of the middle classes when new building materials and techniques produced a totally new universal structure.

This was the age of iron, when an artificial building material was first exploited industrially. The potential of iron was proved in the creation of the railways. Coupled with advances in plate glass manufacture and the introduction of mechanized brick manufacture, the possibilities for large-scale enterprise expanded. Craft firms, out of touch with the scope of increasingly large organizational tasks, eventually gave way to building contractors.

It was an age of change; on a rapid, almost frightening scale. The accustomed way of living was being completely overhauled and architects were scrambling to find an appropriate means of expression for this change.

One building more than any other brought many of these 'discoveries' together and became, in the process, the most flexible innovation of its time. The building was the Crystal Palace, a prefabricated structure built entirely of glass and iron to house the Great Exhibition of 1851 in Hyde Park.

Designed by Joseph Paxton, a self-taught architect who began his career as a gardener, it was a structure of immense size. At six times the size of St Paul's Cathedral, it was able to envelop entire elm trees, and its 800,000 square feet of floor area housed over 100,000 exhibits. Well in excess of six million people wandered through this shining fairy palace in the six months that the exhibition was open.

From Queen to commoner, everyone loved it. And as opposed to St Paul's, which took over 35 years to complete, the Crystal Place took under 35 weeks to construct.

Yet despite its size, it was a truly 'minimal' building in structure and in purpose. As John McKean notes in his book *Crystal Palace*: 'never in human history has so much been written about so little ... so little in terms of so much volume being enclosed with so little mass.' It had one simple *raison d'être* – as spectacle: a magnificent transparent umbrella for the exhibition of wares and discoveries from all over the world. Able to house a crowd larger than any that had ever congregated together before, this enormous structure did not, in its construction, feature any one component weighing more than a ton. Whereas the walls of St Paul's were 14 feet thick, the iron columns of the Crystal Palace were only 8 inches in diameter, conspiring to create a simultaneous impression of monumentality and fragility.

It was Meccano on a heroic scale and it did not fail to impress. Even hardened intellectuals responded in an adolescent fashion, waxing lyrical about this 'modern wonder'. It was the embodiment of modernity, a modernism of clarity, as defined by the French philosopher Montesquieu: 'Everything is visible, everything is available. The heart shows itself as clearly as the face.' Transparency was thus linked to honesty. In building terms, this meant materials should represent what they are and appear to do only what they actually can do. Engineering was for the first time seen as being more honest than architecture.

Here was the credo of today's modern architect resonating around a building of the mid-1800s.

The Crystal Palace provided a precedent for clarity and precision, for a greater appreciation of light and space, and functioned as an encouragement towards embracing and exploring, rather than rejecting, new technology.

If ever a building represented the 'seductive promise' of the Industrial Revolution, this was it.

PREVIOUS PAGE (72)
Designed by Sir George Gilbert Scott, Battersea Power Station is impossible to ignore. Symbol of 1930s industrial power and progress, this imposing building is patiently awaiting a new life. In the meantime it moonlights as an impressive screen for laser-generated advertising images.

OPPOSITE PAGE
Designed to house the Great Exhibition of 1851, the Crystal Palace was the most influential innovation of its time. Built entirely of iron and glass, the prefabricated construction followed no conventional style. Completed in just nine months, it was the world's first 'high-tech' building.

FOLLOWING PAGE (76)
'A temple to imperial consumerism': despite its popularity, the Crystal Palace, erected in Hyde Park, was disassembled and removed shortly after the end of the Great Exhibition. In retrospect it was a masterstroke; the memory of the building remains thus, forever, 'a modern moment'.

BEES

"a fairy palace within walls of iron and glass,

the strongest and most fragile materials

happily and splendidly combined..."

Words from the 13 October *Times* obituary on the Crystal Palace after its closure on 12 October 1851

THE

INTERNATIONAL

STYLE

After the First World War and the Russian Revolution came a revolution of a different kind. An architectural revolution.

In response to the misery and suffering of war and to the complete confusion of Europe's internal order, architects started to see themselves as playing a part in a 'social' revolution. They were, or at least thought they were, pivotal characters in the creation of a new society.

'It is only from the present', they declared, 'that our work should now be derived. And for the first time in history architecture, indeed great architecture, will be concerned with the housing of the ordinary man and woman.' This was architecture with a conscience and it had a name, the International Style, a term coined in 1932 by the organizers of the first international exhibition of modern architecture at the Museum of Modern Art in New York.

The book that accompanied the 1932 exhibition pronounced a new conception of architecture as 'volume rather than mass'. It was architecture on a 'human' and 'humane' level. And because the movement had already declared itself to be concerned only with the present, new technology could be embraced without regard for historical precedent.

It was spearheaded by Le Corbusier, an energetic Swiss architect who created an entirely new way of shaping space. Following the example of Cubist painters, he was the first architect to work within a three-dimensional notion of space, dividing volume both vertically and horizontally at the same time.

Le Corbusier's teaching, writing and work unleashed new possibilities. It was a new frontier for design: architects were now free to consider space or volume as infinite. This was an extraordinary development. Prior to Le Corbusier, architects could move walls, take away furniture and relocate kitchens and bathrooms, but now they had been introduced to the total 'plasticity' of space.

The first and best example of this new freedom in London was Berthold Lubetkin's penguin pool at London Zoo. A Russian émigré, Lubetkin was a keen proponent of reinforced concrete. The poetic and graphic finery of his strong, simple spirals were a most astonishing example of Le Corbusier's teachings. Lubetkin went on to establish the firm Tecton, which was responsible for some of London's most handsome examples of the International Style in reinforced concrete.

It was not until after the Second World War, however, that this new movement really got underway in Britain. The high point was undoubtedly the Festival of Britain in 1951 on the banks of the Thames. It was Britain's post-war 'coming out' party, an exhibition full of expectations of the bright future ahead. It also had political motives. The development of popular American design during the late 1940s and early 1950s horrified the British design establishment, who were attempting, in line with the national character, to promote a more functional style. At the time America was all wings, gadgets and exaggeration. In answer to America's fantasy land, the Council of Industrial Design launched a successful campaign to promote the 'Contemporary Style', which blended the latest developments from America (which after all couldn't be completely ignored) and the sparse simplicity of Swedish design with British traditions. It was a complete success, dominating the Festival. One popular example of this design direction was the Antelope Chair by Ernest Race. With its simple steel rod construction, moulded plywood seat and sensuous organic shape, it was the very definition of post-war optimism.

And it was this optimism that created perhaps the most famous decade in contemporary British history: the 'Swinging Sixties'.

In music, fashion, art and lifestyle, London led the way. It was an atmosphere in which major leaps forward could be made and often were. Apart from the obvious success stories such as Terence Conran's Habitat stores, 1960s boutiques should not be underestimated in their contribution to design. In their attention to packaging and interiors, they raised design to the status of a key commercial constituent of high street activity. Shopping as entertainment had been born.

PREVIOUS PAGE (78)
Some of London's most innovative buildings were built for the Festival of Britain in 1951, including the Lion and Unicorn Pavilion (interior shown here). Held in the centenary year of the Great Exhibition of 1851 on a massive site on the south bank of the Thames, it was briefly Britain's 'modern' moment of glory. Amidst great public protest, the entire site was deconstructed at the close of the Festival.

PREVIOUS PAGES (80–81)
Inspired by Le Corbusier's innovative concept of three-dimensional space, Russian émigré Berthold Lubetkin's 1934 design for the penguin pool at London Zoo was one of the first and most dramatic examples of the poetic potential of steel-reinforced concrete. Berthold Lubetkin, who later went on to found Tecton, designed what must surely rank as the most sophisticated animal house in any zoo.

OPPOSITE PAGE
'Girl in plastic miniskirt', a metaphor for the contribution of 'Swinging Sixties' London to design. Boutiques like Mary Quant, in their attention to packaging, interiors and graphics, raised design to a new status as a key component of commercial success and in the process brought it more mainstream than ever before. They broke with virtually all standing traditions, and made it fashionable to do so.

3

COLOURS

Colour plays a distinct role in shaping the visual culture of a city or country. It is one of the oldest forms of communication known, and we are attracted to it like magpies to a shiny object. Colour is simple and pure.

In 1924, the Post Office launched a competition for the design of a telephone kiosk. The clear winner was Sir George Gilbert Scott. As John Timpson describes in his book *Requiem for a Red Box*: 'the judges took one look at it and ran singing and dancing into the streets.' K2, as Scott's winning design unceremoniously came to be known (literally, Kiosk no. 2), was an architectural delight. It was the epitome of classicism. It was also a perfect synthesis of form and function.

Built of cast iron with a teak door and a concrete base, its sheer mass made it almost impossible to damage. Yet, despite its hefty construction, it had a refined appearance. A reeded Grecian surround distinguished the door, the glass panes were glazed in a manner not unlike the windows of London's Georgian houses, and the square pillar shape was elegantly finished with a dome made of segmented curves. Ventilation was ingeniously provided by a stylized perforated crown punched into the curve sections. Perhaps a lot of this refinement was lost on a public mainly interested in making a phone call, but K2 was practical too. For the caller's convenience it was rainproof, draughtproof and very nearly soundproof. Painted 'Post Office Red' it was easy to spot.

In all, 76,500 of Scott's telephone kiosks were introduced to Britain. Very few Britons alive today can remember life without them. They are now so much a part of the British way of life that they have been listed as heritage sites.

The 'red box' was an architectural masterpiece: a successful distillation of a comprehensive series of requirements, executed in a distinctly British and, dare I say it, minimal manner.

PREVIOUS PAGE (86)
'Post Office Red'. Nowhere in the world has this one colour been used so effectively in establishing an unmistakable public code. It has helped the mail boxes, telephone booths and buses of London to become international icons – an exercise in communication minimalism.

PREVIOUS PAGE (88)
'Silver quilting' of the Thames Flood Barrier. Designed by the engineering firm of Rendel, Palmer and Tritton, the construction is an answer to London's threat of being flooded. (The city has sunk 15 feet since Roman times.) The elegantly shaped forms, clad in panels of stainless steel, house electro-hydraulic units capable of lifting four gates of 3,000 tons, lying on the river bed, into position in case the water level rises too high.

PREVIOUS PAGE (89)
Throughout London, mews houses, once coach houses or stables, have been targets for renovation. In this particular case, the distinctive and original tongue and groove stable doors were retained when the former inner-city dairy was converted into a minimal boutique called 'Egg'.

OPPOSITE PAGE
In the late spring many of London's inner-city residential streets turn into grand parades of white blossom. Where trees face each other on either side of the road, entire gateways of these cool, off-white blossoms can be found. But nature is sparing and the entire spectacle lasts for no longer than two weeks of the year.

FOOD MARK

eurostar
3006
HARVEY NICHOLS
ROSEHIPS AND HIBISCUS
25 HERBAL TEA BAGS
net wt 62.5g 2.2oz e
HARVEY NICHOLS
WILD CHERRY
25 FRUIT TEA BAGS
net wt 62.5g 2.2oz e
HARVEY NICHOLS
PEPPERMINT
25 HERBAL TEA BAGS
net wt 37.5g 1.32oz e

1	2	3	4
5	6	7	8
9	10	11	12
13	14	15	16

PHOTOS IN ORDER OF APPEARANCE – PREVIOUS PAGES (92–93)

1 & 16

One of the most design-conscious department stores in the world, Harvey Nichols has applied distinct and minimal graphic styles to the trademark silver packaging of their own brand.

2

The pristine white Design Museum is the brain child of design entrepreneur Terence Conran. A new landmark in Docklands, it serves as a venue for exhibitions and debates on design.

3

Slim vertical blinds play a distinct role in London's new minimalism. Rather than only covering a window, they cover an entire wall and the window forms a pattern as on a projection screen.

4

White houses, with Georgian proportions punctuated by neatly repetitive windows in classical shapes, and black doors constitute the familiar and much-loved architectural discipline of London.

5

Given the uniform discipline of London's terrace houses, fanlight windows above the doorways provide perhaps the only opportunity for decorative individuality.

6

A shop called Egg. Created by Maureen Dogherty in an old inner London dairy, Egg is an example of a minimal approach to interior design that is nonetheless soft and inviting.

7 & 9

Egg's old dairy barn door shows how proprietor and designer Maureen Dogherty applied a clear, simple sense of purpose without sacrificing the characteristic original features.

8

London's Architectural Association has consistently turned out some of the world's finest architects. This 1930s photo is a reminder of the English love of order and restraint.

10

A strong sense of clarity is a trademark of English design, including graphics. London ad agencies consistently produce some of the most striking, powerful work, as exemplified by outdoor billboard posters.

11 & 12

The new Waterloo Eurostar terminal, designed by London architect Nick Grimshaw, continues the English tradition of celebrating technological advances with powerful and progressive architecture.

13

A detail of a typical London iron picket fence with its 'Etruscan spears' reveals the rich compendium of shapes and symbols from the classics that constitute London's distinct visual landscape.

14

The food market at Harvey Nichols, designed entirely in expanses of silver and white, is clean, modern and minimal. It breaks with all traditions since it is located on the roof as opposed to in the basement.

15

Britain was the first nation since Roman times to introduce central heating. A hundred years later the ubiquitous radiator has become a genuine British icon – a symbol of the positive contribution of the Industrial Revolution.

OPPOSITE PAGE

Sir George Gilbert Scott's design for the K2, the world's most famous telephone booth, is dwarfed by his other creation, the Battersea Power Station.

TELEPHONE
TELEPHONE

4

INGREDIENTS

Design is like a language. It is often specific to a place and its overall culture. The same symbols and patterns resurface in different forms and styles and they serve as both the source and the result of creative inspiration.

deux

2 Trom

2 Haut

ns, Alto, B

2 Cors, 2

ettes & Timbal

Composée par

Bassons

W. A. MOZAR

de Sinfonie

pour

Alto, Basse,

deux Vio

Alto, Basse,

Grande Sinfonie

Alto Basse

deux Violons, Alto Basse,

Alto, Basse

2

ns, A

MOZA

2

ande Sin

Grande Sinfonie

GOLDEN

GIRL

Textiles are a British institution.

At one time the wealth of the Empire was dependent on the output of the newly industrialized centres such as Manchester, where vast quantities of textiles of all descriptions were able to be churned out thanks to Britain's newest invention: mass production. The Industrial Revolution took the world by storm and Britain's dominance in the rag trade was for a time unassailable. One of the reasons for British prominence was the manufacturers' ability to absorb all manner of styles and influences and then re-export them in a slightly different form, establishing a trend for their 'new' creations which they had in fact copied from elsewhere.

So cleverly and convincingly was this done that no one today would credit chintz, that most British of British fabrics, as originating from India. Chintz started life as *chint*, colourful cottons decorated with handblock-printed patterns, a tradition almost as old as India itself. It was all the rage when it was first brought to Britain and the home mills were not slow to start making their own versions.

Britain's dominance of the textile industry has long since faded and today's mainstream fabric industry, like the automobile industry, is dominated by a few large multinationals. Interestingly, this rationalization of the industry has created an important niche for small craft textile studios.

At this more creative and expressive end of the textile market Britain is once again dominant. In the world of decorative textiles, many small design studios, such as Designers Guild, Osborne and Little, and Colefax and Fowler, have become internationally recognized and even quite famous despite the relatively small quantity of actual textile sales. They are the 'fashion house' equivalents in the world of design and decoration.

One designer has created more interest in this arena recently than any other. Carolyn Quartermaine has had an unprecedented amount of publicity about her work – sensuous fabrics adorned by her unique and expressive calligraphy. Fabric creations that are pure and simple.

The inclusion of a designer who works in decorative textiles may seem an odd, if not incongruous, choice for a book entitled *London Minimum*, but her work does in fact share the qualities that define the interests of this book. Quartermaine's fabrics have the essential hallmarks, namely clarity and restraint.

Like a true artist she has concentrated on one thing, and she continues to strive to get it just right. In this she is steadfast. Her work remains firmly rooted in the two ingredients she has brought together so successfully: fabric and calligraphy. Her individual creations are meant to be used sparingly, just a single cushion in a room. In this manner the work transcends the purely decorative genre.

Minimalism is not about living in an empty house. It is about applying standards as a way of fighting against a consumer society that continually shrieks at us to 'buy! buy! buy!' Inevitably people end up with a lot of junk that they neither use nor admire. The main challenge of minimalism is 'Why put up with it? Think and decide what is useful, important and beautiful and get rid of the rest.'

Quartermaine's creations follow this very line of thought. She has reduced her own expression to a manner that suits her aesthetic sense. She is not concerned with coming up with a new range for every selling season, nor is she interested in fads or fashions. She does what she finds to be beautiful and doesn't give a damn if others don't care for it. Her work has integrity and discipline, key words in the whole minimal approach.

As she says: 'I am 100% a visual person. That is why I've banned the *banal* from my view. I don't want to see Fairy Liquid and dishwashing brushes. I want to see gold plates in pristine white spaces.' Living and working are inseparable for Carolyn Quartermaine. For her, life is aesthetic expression – full time.

"A style is not a style until it has its beauty.
But the beauty is born of necessity; it is not an arbitary choice; it is
rather the exact solution of a problem."

Herbert Read

PREVIOUS PAGE (98)
Quartermaine's fabrics are the essence of simplicity. Just two ingredients are the hallmarks of her exquisite work: fine, carefully selected textiles and her elegant flowing calligraphy. Art as textile? Or textile as art?

PREVIOUS PAGES (100–101)
London is seen as the hub of the world of decorative textiles, and amongst its vast array of fabric houses Quartermaine's work is the most refined. These are works of compact preciousness, the truffles of textiles: they have a power that can best be appreciated in a restrained context. The effect they have is simultaneously rich and minimal.

OPPOSITE PAGE
Carolyn Quartermaine has become something of a golden girl in design circles. She has had an extraordinary amount of publicity and yet her work remains fresh. The secret of her success lies in her individual response to each piece of fabric. For her, no two pieces are ever the same.

PARED DOWN PIECES

In 1986, Sheridan Coakley took a stand at the hugely influential Milan Furniture Fair and launched the designs of a handful of young, unknown English designers. It was a huge success. English design brought a fresh simplicity back to the design arena. It was a welcome relief from Italian design, which was increasingly burdened by obscure intellectual approaches. Ten years on, these English designers have become household names and their work dominates the catalogues of many of the most upmarket Italian manufacturers. Their rise has marked the revival, at last, of a long-standing English tradition. A tradition of making beautiful furniture.

Much of the furniture that captured the headlines of the 1980s was an expression of extravagance, of flamboyant invention with prices to match. But now, all that ostentation looks increasingly out of keeping with the mood of the times. A primary concern for clarity has resurfaced, clarity in form as well as function. These are pieces that rely on the beauty of natural, untreated timber and on clean, simple lines. No tricks. Balance and beauty are once again, after a long absence, part of cutting-edge design. Design entrepreneur Sheridan Coakley came onto the scene at exactly the right time.

Since his first Milan Furniture Fair in 1986, Coakley and his firm SCP have been responsible for introducing the designs of Jasper Morrison, Matthew Hilton, Nigel Coates and, more recently, Konstantin Grcic and Terence Woodgate. Like Terence Conran, Coakley operates on 'intuition'. His decisions are guided by his own taste, which is quite English. He doesn't like what Matthew Hilton calls 'arty farty' furniture and he doesn't like things that are gimmicky. He likes furniture that is innovative and classic, utilizing the latest technology but based in history.

Just about the only English designer Coakley didn't discover was Tom Dixon, who seems to have done a pretty good job of that himself. Unlike Morrison, Grcic and Irvine, who all graduated from the Royal College of Art, Dixon is largely self-taught and self-invented. After a brief stint at Chelsea Art School, which he left because 'it had so little to offer', he made a name for himself welding scrap metal on stage at the Titanic Club. It was the kind of performance art one would expect to find in a futuristic film. This eventually led to the Creative Salvage Movement and welding scrap metal to make 'things'. Dixon's approach has always been one of energetic experimentation and as such he has worked in just about every medium and on every

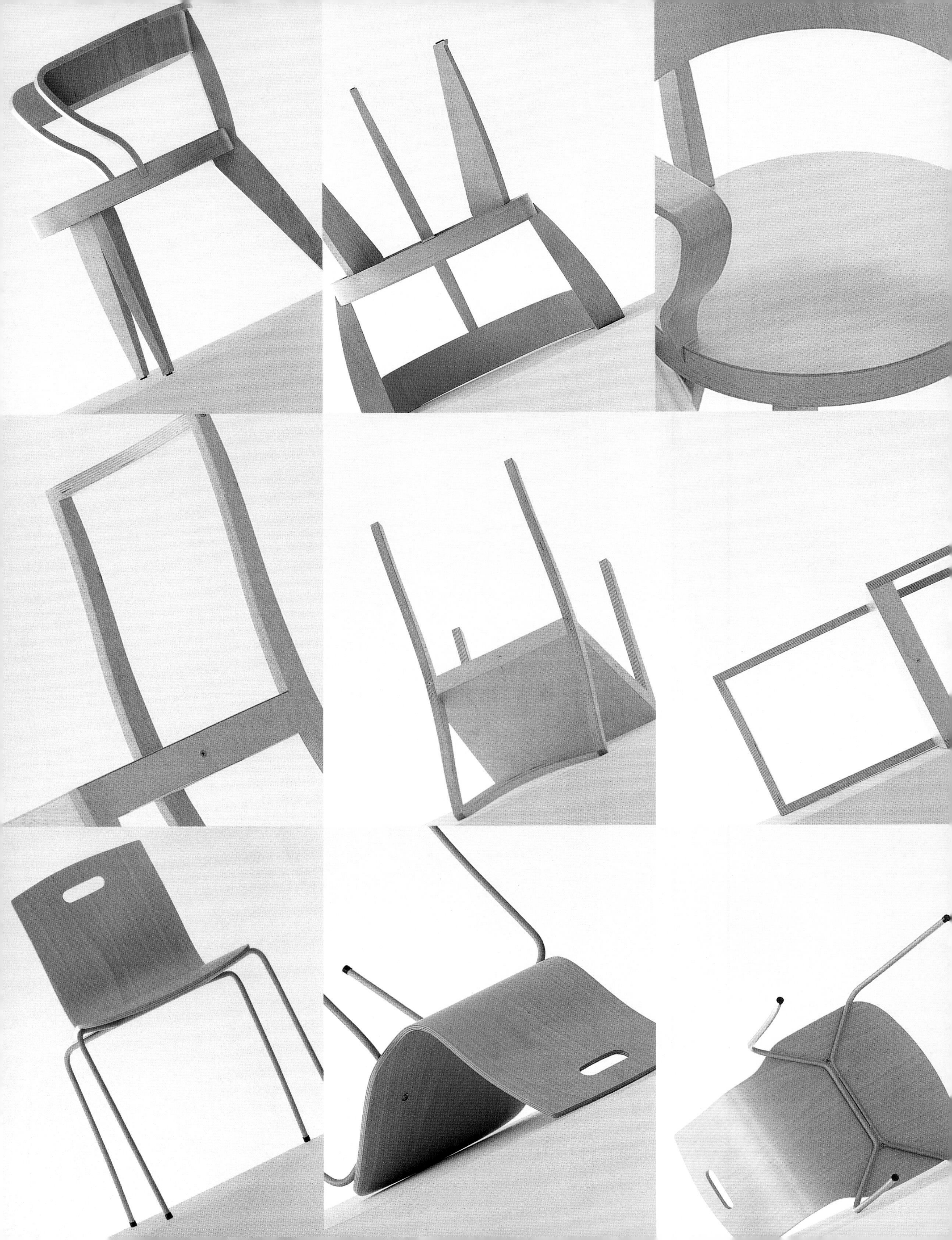

subject matter. It was almost inevitable that from such a prolific approach the odd 'classic' would emerge: for instance, the cantilever 'S' chair, designed in 1987 and now produced by Cappellini in Italy, is both elaborately decorative and remarkably simple. Like a true classic, it cuts across the usual boundaries of popular taste.

If Tom Dixon is the most colourful of England's new crop of furniture designers, then Jasper Morrison is the most monochrome. His softly spoken designs reduce form and technology to almost childlike simplicity in both appearance and the manner in which they are made. He is the most 'minimal' of the bunch but his sparse pieces are certainly not without style. On the contrary, they are compelling because they make such sophisticated use of one ingredient, namely restraint.

Another English designer close to the world of industrial design is James Irvine. Irvine left London in 1984 to work in the Olivetti design studio in Milan and, except for a year in design research with Toshiba in Tokyo, he has remained there. He is now a partner of Sottsass Associati and works for, amongst others, Alessi, Abet Laminati, Cappellini, Vitra and, of course, Sheridan Coakley's SCP.

Irvine has the sophistication of a designer who moves in powerful circles, and the result, interestingly enough, of all this experience and exposure is a strong respect for the value of clarity. As he says: 'It's not easy to do a project which is clear and without tricks. The idea of the creative *gesture* is all very well but if the object survives more by gesture, rather than for what it does, then it is art, and only few, very few, gestures become great art.'

"The practical commonsense of modern society ... is the natural genius of the British mind... The bias of the nation is a passion for utility."

Ralph Waldo Emerson

PREVIOUS PAGE (104)
Tom Dixon's 'S' chair has become a modern classic. Designed in 1988, the chair combines simplicity with modern engineering and organic form. Dixon, with his SCP colleagues, has joined an elite band of British furniture designers whose designs are now being manufactured by various international firms including Cappellini of Italy.

PREVIOUS PAGES (106–107)
Chairs by Jasper Morrison and James Irvine. Not too long ago all the output of hip, design-conscious manufacturers in Italy was dominated by Italian names. Now, the balance has shifted somewhat. A new style has emerged out of London which is the antithesis of the anarchic, histrionic designs of the Italians. They are minimal designs: minimal in line, minimal in colour and minimal in material. These are chairs on a diet: slim, streamlined and devoid of any decorative 'fat'.

OPPOSITE PAGE
James Irvine's chair combines the pared-down palette of British design with the deeply ingrained Italian respect for the classics. A successful example of British sobriety and Latin flair coming together.

SIMPLE

SILVER

SERVICE

There is, in the words of design author Stephen Bayley, 'something essentially English about the character of David Mellor's designs: they are elegant but understated, strong in character, but unobtrusive'.

Not unexpectedly, Mellor was influenced and inspired by Georgian silver.

The revolution in taste introduced by the influx of Huguenot artisans was as dramatic for silverware as it was for the development of English furniture. New standards were set in technical as well as stylistic terms. At first there was a considerable gap separating the skills and preferences of English craftsmen and those of their more flamboyant Huguenot colleagues; but with time, and particularly in what became known as 'utilitarian style', they were able to synthesize their skills and talents. Sauceboats, teapots, coffeepots and even forks and spoons were characterized by carefully balanced proportions and an austere plainness that was considered, even by fans of more ornamental work, to be 'perfectly appropriate'.

Perhaps the most fundamental innovation of early 18th-century dining plate was the matched table service. Sets of spoons had been known for centuries but until this time the notion of matching knife, spoon and fork and repeating the same in smaller sizes for fruit and dessert was a completely new concept.

Silver had been something collected piece by individual piece and the only consistency had been in the choice of artisan commissioned to make it. Sameness did not become part of the brief until Georgian times, when the drive to standardize in the building industry eventually filtered right down to the chairs and tables of the dining room and even to the table silver.

Unlike any silversmith before him, David Mellor has combined the major strands in English silverware history to create cutlery that has achieved both commercial and critical success. Mellor has forged together the classicism of Georgian style and the industrial developments of Victorian times with the lightness, slimness and precision of modern design.

Mellor was born in Sheffield in 1930 and educated at the Sheffield College of Art, the Royal College of Art in London and the British School in Rome. In 1954 he

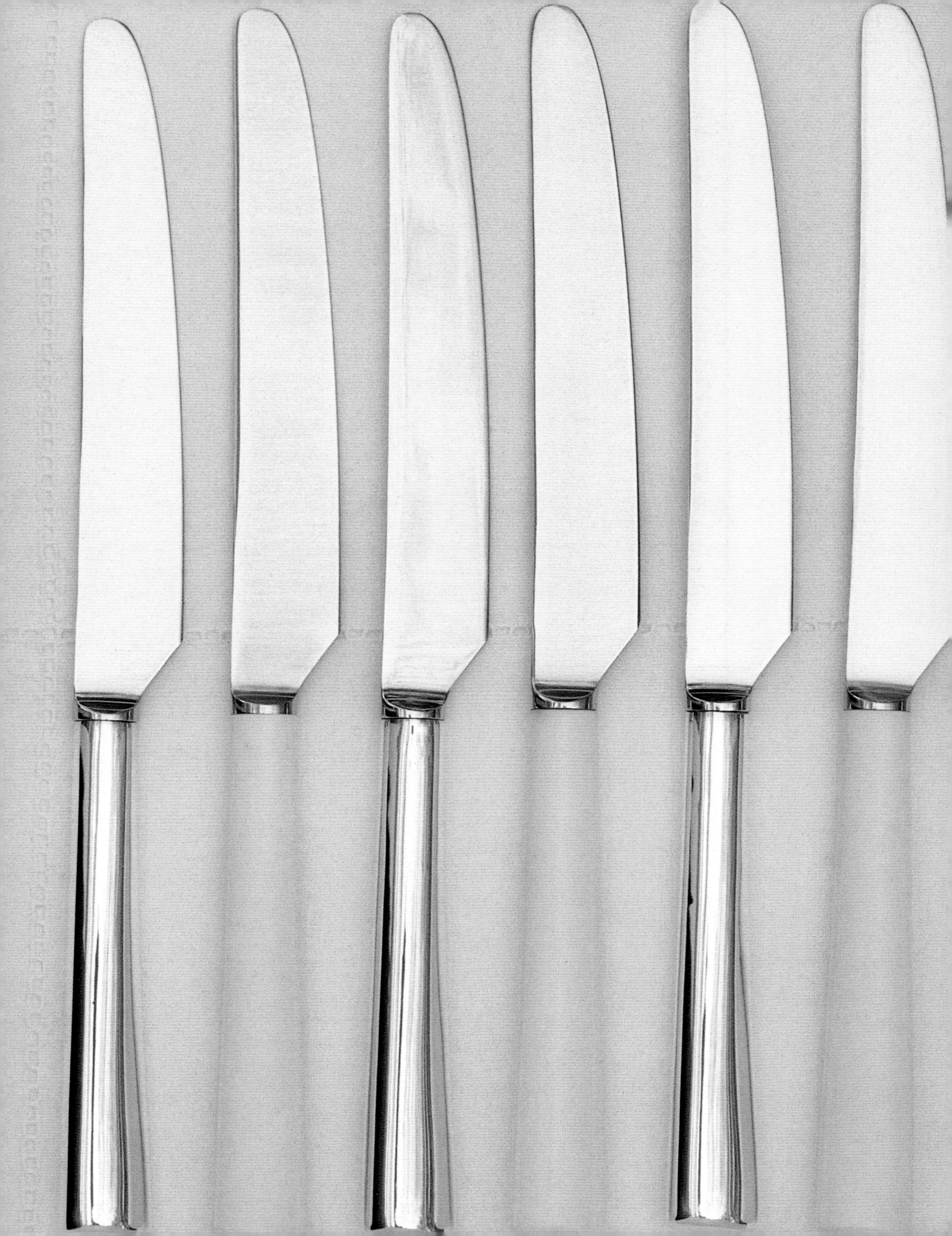

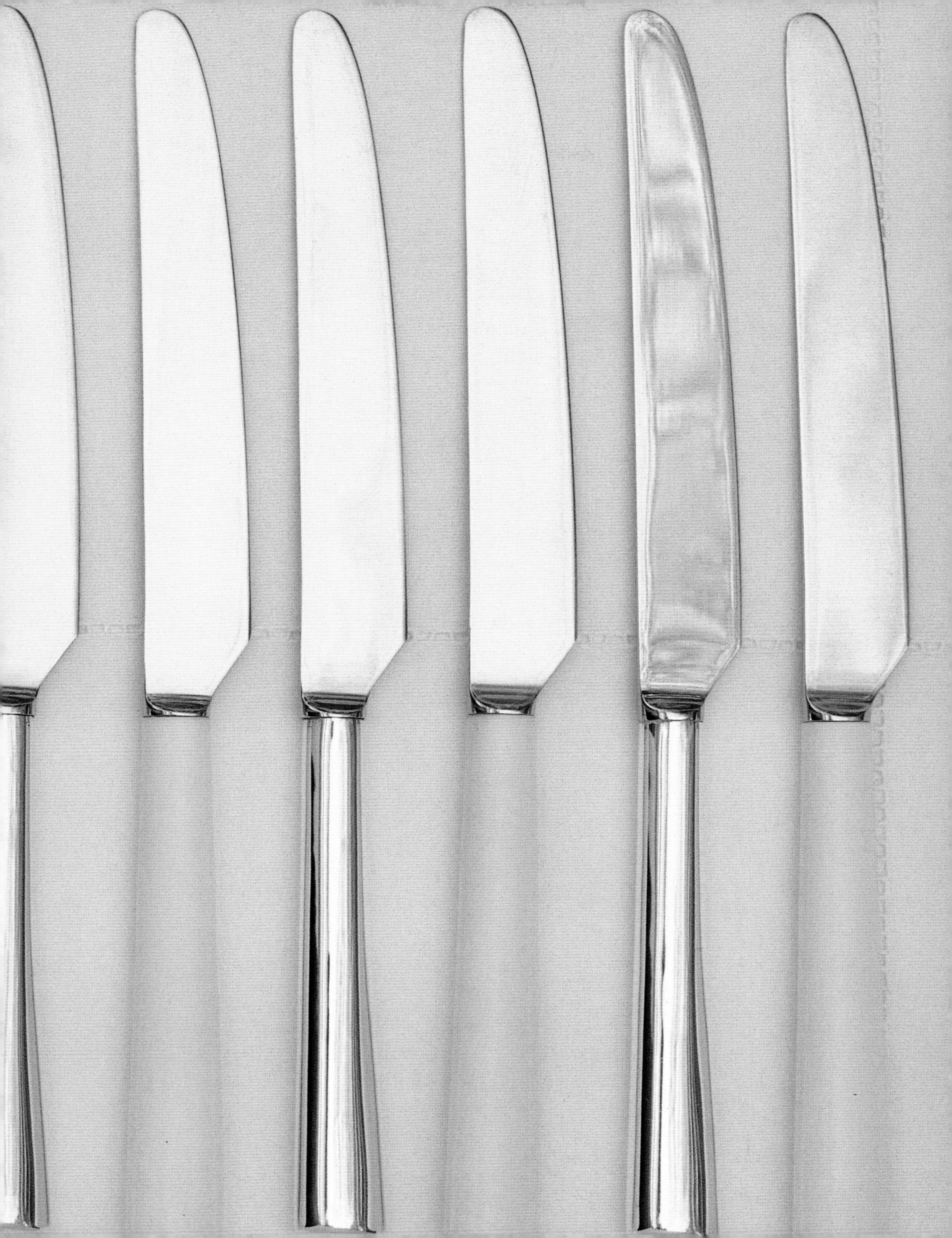

opened a design office and workshop in Sheffield. His range and output as an industrial designer have been considerable, including telephones, street lighting, furniture and special commissions such as a candelabra for Goldsmiths' Hall and a bronze fountain for the Botanical Gardens in Cambridge. But it is in silverware, and especially cutlery, that he has found his true métier. Originally trained as a silversmith, Mellor brings a craftsman's eye to his design and a designer's discipline to his craft. He sees design as a far broader issue than just being concerned with 'making things'. More important, he feels, is 'making choices', choosing how we want to live: a concern, it seems, shared by most protagonists of minimalism.

He is also straightforward about the need for design to be more commercially motivated. He has no time for designers who complain about lack of financial success. 'Perhaps', he says, 'they should be more entrepreneurial.'

Being a design entrepreneur has certainly worked for Mellor. He is a trustee of the Victoria and Albert Museum and has held the post of chairman of the Design Council Committee reporting on British design. In 1963 he won the commission to design *Embassy*, a silver service for use in all British embassies. He is also the proprietor of two high-profile kitchen 'equipment' emporia, one in London and one in Manchester, which sell pared-down culinary tools together with the full range of his cutlery designs. But perhaps his greatest single statement of success is his award-winning *Pride*. Strongly influenced by Georgian silver, Mellor's most successful design was included in the 1957 Design Centre Awards and it has been going strong ever since. Apart from having its handles made dishwasher-proof, it has hardly changed. It is featured in the collections of the Victoria and Albert Museum, the Worshipful Company of Goldsmiths and the Museum of Modern Art, New York. With *Pride* David Mellor has achieved perhaps the ultimate designers' accolade: the creation of a 'modern design classic'.

PREVIOUS PAGE (110)
A design tribute to the creative talent of the turn-of-the-century 'Wiener Werkstätte', and in particular to architect Josef Hoffmann. Manufactured from 18/8 stainless steel, its visual character comes from subtle gradations of thickness previously only found in hand-forged Georgian silver.

PREVIOUS PAGES (112–113)
Described by Peter Dormer, author of Design since 1945, *as 'arguably the finest cutlery design of the past hundred years',* Pride *has been a critical and commercial success since it was first released in 1954. It is in the permanent collections of New York's MOMA and London's V&A.*

OPPOSITE PAGE
Appropriately named English, *David Mellor's newest cutlery design goes back to tradition for its inspiration. Mellor's drawing upon the qualities of early Georgian silver – concern for balance, form and utility – has resulted in a design that is classic, yet quite minimal in its lack of decoration.*

CRAFT OF CLARITY

Ray Key is a wood-turner. A poet in wood. Using nothing more than a single material and a simple shape, he makes items of exquisite beauty. Like the writer who can muster emotion from the right words used sparingly, Key can create visual drama with a single block of wood.

His pieces have the power of clarity.

Looking at them, the entire notion of minimalism becomes much easier to understand. By eliminating all distractions he allows the true attraction of the material to surface. All the natural, inherent beauty that wood has to offer is magnified by the completely naked honesty of his work. Yet Key's is probably the most demanding of paths to choose because it is so unforgiving. There is no room for mistakes. The work must be precise and flawless, otherwise the eye is distracted. In Japan they have a word for it, *Wabi*, a word that literally means 'voluntary poverty'. It derives from the teachings of Buddha which specify that man should strive for 'poverty', in the sense of being 'thingless', because to be thingless is to possess the world. For a bowl or whatever object to have *Wabi* it must be pure – in form, material and execution. In Zen philosophy, the ultimate goal is 'stillness and simplicity'. If an object is deemed to have *Wabi* this represents the ultimate compliment because it has transcended mere beauty and attained a spiritual quality.

There are, it seems, no short cuts to this kind of perfection.

It takes dedication and persistence, and Ray Key has been at it for over thirty years. As with most things of apparent simplicity, Key's pieces seem effortless. They are, after all, so simple. Yet in reality the path to achieving these results is a complex and arduous one. Key's commitment starts at the mill. He makes his own selection and marks directly onto the log which sections he wants cut. Experience and an innate understanding of the material, not to mention his fair share of previous mistakes, mean that Key can confidently pick out the quality of grain that he is after from logs that have not yet been near a saw. Upon his instructions the sawyers will cut a 'plank' measuring 12 feet long, 6 inches thick and 4 feet wide: a single piece of wet wood weighing more than a ton. (Timber is milled soaking wet because it is so

much easier to cut.) This olive ash 'monolith' is then further cut into three 4-foot lengths and halved down the middle. The end result of a few days at the mill is six pieces of wood 4 feet long, 2 feet wide and a whopping 6 inches thick. These are the blocks from which he will sculpt his pristine, unadorned bowls. After each bowl has been rough-turned (again from timber that is still wet) it is left to dry for eight to ten weeks. Then all that remains is the final turning. Along the way Key has, like the craftsmen of old, controlled every step, from the choice of wood to the manner of its cutting, drying, aging and storing; a process of exacting standards and discipline.

It is fascinating to contemplate that items such as his large-diameter bowls are solid fragments of trees that have been growing for two, three or even four hundred years. Perhaps that is one of the reasons he is so careful. Unlike veneer, which in a sense is a sort of destruction of the basic material, an item of solid wood is something that will last for generations: a botanical wonder becoming more beautiful with each passing day.

"When is the rest of the furniture coming?"

Doris Saatchi
on people's first reaction to her minimalist home

PREVIOUS PAGE (116)
Carved from a single piece of silver ash, Ray Key's bowls epitomize the minimal approach to design. Pared down to a point where it can no longer be improved upon, its beauty lies purely in its shape and the quality of the material itself. It has no decorative detailing to camouflage any imperfection – this can be seen to reflect the fundamental basis of Zen philosophy known as Wabi, *a quest for 'voluntary poverty'.*

PREVIOUS PAGES (118–119)
Since Elizabethan times timber has played a role in England's design history. The different periods of English history can be charted by the wood preferences of each era. Elizabethan times were the age of oak, Queen Anne's brief reign can be seen as the age of walnut and Georgian England emerged as the age of mahogany. The 20th century is the age of light timbers. Blond woods have become the preferred choice for modern interiors.

OPPOSITE PAGE
'Imago nova mundi, imago nulla' *(To imagine something new in the world is to imagine nothing). Interestingly, the majority of minimal pieces, from chairs to bowls, for all that they give the impression of being 'modern', are essentially derived from classical shapes and forms. A historical pedigree combined with a careful attention to quality ensure that pieces such as Ray Key's bowls will one day be seen as a 'modern' design classic.*

NEUTRAL

NATURALS

Of all the design disciplines, rug design has probably seen the least innovation. Yet the minimal approach has, if anything, created a stronger demand for the work.

Christopher Farr was one of the first to recognize the potential in this specialized area of interior design. He understood that people opting for hard floors together with a more pared-down approach to furnishing were creating a vast natural backdrop on which a rug of real integrity and beauty would stand out.

Trained in fine art at the Chelsea School of Art and the Slade School, Farr's interest in modern art, and in American painting of the 1950s and 1960s in particular (Pollock, Noland, Stella, Motherwell and Judd amongst others), was given a twist by the three months he spent in Peru on a Boise Travelling Scholarship in 1975. Intense exposure to Pre-Columbian art awakened a passion for colour-saturated textiles that would prove to be a major influence on all that followed. For several years he worked with David Black, the pioneering West London rug dealer, further improving his knowledge of tribal and indigenous textiles, as well as teaching painting at the Byam Shaw School of Art. Then in 1988 he struck out on his own and established Christopher Farr Handmade Rugs. Though he initially specialized in antique carpets and tribal rugs, the success of a joint project with the Royal College of Art entitled *Brave New Rugs* convinced him to embark in a new and unique direction. For the first time he could bring together the two predominant passions in his life: modern art and traditional indigenous handcraft. Thus was launched an innovative approach to rugs that combined the talents of select 'artists' with the superb, traditional craft methods of the weavers and dyers in Konya, central Turkey.

One of the most memorable of these creative ventures was the rug designs of Romeo Gigli. Long recognized as the 'texture' genius of Italian fashion, Gigli brought his extraordinary eye for colour, sheen and all the other tactile qualities of fabric to what would ultimately become an exquisite range of rugs. Hand-knotted by villagers in Konya, all the yarns were painstakingly chosen from a large selection of specially created colours.

The success of the Gigli rugs and other similar ventures no doubt inspired Farr to return to his training and his artistic roots to produce works of his own design. With great clarity and restraint, he has designed a range that in many ways is the equivalent in rugs to the minimalist approach in interiors and architecture. It's a subtle approach both in pattern and texture. Unlike the tribal rugs that he bought and sold early in his career, Farr's own designs rely on a predominance of neutral tonings and minimal, abstract patterning.

Farr's own formative influences are brought to these rugs in a careful, almost concealed manner. If one were not familiar with his passion for the work of Motherwell, for instance, then one of his designs, which features broad bands of neutral shades interrupted by the most discreet lines of blue, could be seen as a simple geometric pattern, nothing more. This potential ambiguity is exactly, one suspects, what Farr was striving for. Obviousness does not play a role. Neither does preciousness. Despite their handmade beauty these rugs were intended for use on the floor. He doesn't even seem too upset at the thought of people putting furniture on them.

Christopher Farr has brought together two worlds, the purity of the abstract expression of so-called naive primitives and the painting, sculpture and architecture of the 20th century. This is a new way of looking at the handcraft of central Turkey.

In the absence of traditional motifs, symbols and patterns the eye can focus on the superb texture that results from the hand-knotting skill. The uneven sheen of the slightly undulating hand-trimmed pile is a jewel-like quality that, luckily, could never be duplicated on a machine.

This is a different kind of luxury. It is not screaming 'look at me'; rather, it indulges the senses in the same manner as a long slab of polished marble or an immaculately laid timber floor. It is all about sensual, tactile simplicity.

PREVIOUS PAGE (122)
Originally specializing in antique carpets and rugs, Christopher Farr first came to the attention of the design world with an exhibition called Brave New Rugs, *a highly successful collaboration with the Royal College of Art. Since then he has worked with the internationally renowned fashion designer Romeo Gigli, amongst others, and has, in the process, become the market-leader in contemporary rugs.*

PREVIOUS PAGES (124–125)
This latest range marks the occasion of the first rugs of his own design being marketed. Working from a palette of neutral shades and pure primary colours, designer Christopher Farr was concerned to create rugs that would work in today's interiors. Given the modern preference for hard floors of stone or timber, these rugs follow the same minimal thinking: quality of detailing, subtlety of approach and concern for visual calm.

OPPOSITE PAGE
Entirely hand-knotted, Farr's rugs, made using the methods of the weavers and dyers of Konya in central Turkey, benefit from the perfection of imperfection. The slightly uneven trimming of the pile creates beautiful plays of light and the density of the knotting provides a lush luxuriousness no machine-made rug could match. In the absence of tribal patterning and other dominant motifs, the superb texture becomes more noticeable.

5

VIRTUOSI

In music, in art, in almost every human creative endeavour, there are always people who stand out, people whose achievements warrant focus and attention. They often establish new directions and create pioneering approaches; they are leaders – they are the virtuosi in their chosen field of expertise.

MR

MINIMUM

JOHN PAWSON

Much has been written about John Pawson's work. It evokes strong reactions: people either hate it or they love it.

Perhaps it's the arrogance of it all. His work has no social agenda. He is not trying to solve problems or deal with the practical concerns that the average architect has to tackle. Architecture is his life, not his career, and he does it mainly to please himself. He does not seem concerned if his approach is understood or accepted and he enjoys the luxury of always having clients. All he is concerned with is, as he says, 'cutting out the crap'.

For him, it's all rather simple and straightforward: 'Architecture is about space; space qualified by light, geometry and repetition ... with the key element being restraint.' And restraint is something he takes very seriously indeed.

Empty houses, it seems, make most people quite anxious. They associate physical softness with emotional comfort. Pawson will have none of it. He is convinced that the epitome of modern luxury is space and light – providing a calm that contrasts with the chaos of the city. Pawson's architecture is all about lifting the sense of oppression that comes from 'clutter' by reducing a space and its contents to the barest minimum.

In the art world this minimalism has become a widely accepted and powerful approach. Towards the end of his career Mark Rothko said he hoped his paintings would ultimately resemble the sides of a tent. Yves Klein made a big name and reputation with just one colour now known as Yves Klein blue.

In architecture minimalism has not yet reached the same level of understanding. Despite a lot of attention from the press, the general impression usually created is of a bizarre spectacle, the result of 'Oh my God! How can people live like this?'-type reporting. This may sell newspapers but it misses the point. It's all about adults making adult choices. As Cindy Palmano, a noted photographer and enthusiast for Pawson's work, points out: 'Its like asking how you walk in platform shoes – comfort and easiness are not the main concern ... What matters with Pawson's work is the mood his spaces put one in – tranquil, contemplative, elegant.'

Pawson can be said to be an architect of the extreme. He will do whatever it takes to follow his singular vision. His own house in London's Notting Hill is the best example. From the outside the standard Victorian row house gives very little away. Unlike its seemingly identical neighbours, the interior couldn't be more different: it is a paragon of reduction.

There are no paintings, pictures or drawings on the walls; no rugs, carpets or mats on the floors; no curtains, drapes or shutters on the windows. No visible taps, switches, latches or knobs. No skirting boards or doorjambs. No sofas, easy chairs or daybeds. No books. No antiques. No *things*. Just space and light. All symmetry and geometry in eye-soothing shades of blond and white.

Pawson has used his house as an arena, a place to work with new ideas and notions, a place to push the envelope of reduction even further.

The floorboards are a perfect example. They have to be the widest boards used in modern times. Combined with the fact that they run unbroken the entire length of the house, they create the impression that the entire tree has been brought into the house (which isn't far from the truth). The specially selected Douglas fir trees were grown in Germany, shipped to Denmark to be specially milled and then transported to London in 45-foot lengths. The stools and the table, constructed on site from the same timber as the floorboards, provide a tactile reminder of the 'chunky' scale of these wooden 'runners'. Together with a couple of 1930s ladderback chairs by Danish designer Kaare Klint, they constitute the only furniture in the house.

"God is in the details."

Mies van der Rohe

PREVIOUS PAGE (130)
The conversion of John Pawson's own home, a Victorian terrace in London's Notting Hill, provided the opportunity to put some new ideas to the test. Most pronounced of these was the choice of floor. Boards of Douglas fir were laid the entire length of the house in unbroken planks, all the more remarkable considering their extreme width. This is a solid timber floor like no other. The bed, stools and 10-foot dining table were made on site. The simple stools are a good indication of the massive size of the floorboards. The fireplace, remodelled from the Victorian original, and the stone bench repeat eye-pleasing planes of pure geometry.

PREVIOUS PAGES (132–133)
The two reception rooms have been transformed into one space, retaining both working fireplaces. On the opposite wall a row of pivoting doors conceal storage space. The structural downstand beam was made deliberately deep to retain at least a suggestion of two spaces.

OPPOSITE PAGE
Pawson's trademark staircase. Set in a narrow vertical space between two walls, the steps do not touch the walls, creating the impression of a floating staircase. Elegance is the key to these details. Ordinary aspects of a house that never usually attract any attention suddenly take on a visual status of their own.

1	2	3	4
5	6	7	8

PHOTOS IN ORDER OF APPEARANCE – PREVIOUS PAGES (136–137)

1

A monastic dining table, a long bench and two ladderback chairs constitute the only 'furniture' in the main living area of John Pawson's own home. All bric-a-brac is hidden behind floor-to-ceiling flush-mounted white doors along one wall.

2

A singularly impressive distinction of this impressive space is the fact that the floorboards run in one continuous length from the front to the rear. The kitchen is a visual extension of the main space, cleverly terminated by a wall of glass.

3

The choice of furniture within such a refined space was subjected to rigorous standards in terms of quality and restraint. One chair that measures up is the ladderback chair designed by Hans Wegner.

4

Le Corbusier once said that the eye is naturally drawn to geometric shapes such as squares, circles, spheres and pyramids. John Pawson put the theory to the test in his own house. The sink is cut from a single solid block of stone.

5

The kitchen counter top consists of a single piece of white Carrara marble that had to be lowered into place by a crane. It is of sufficient depth for a shallow sink to have been cut directly from the slab. The vola tap is wall-mounted to avoid clutter.

6

Only three materials have been allowed into the house, namely: stone, timber and white-painted plaster. The fireplace, one of two, is original to the house. The horizontal profile mimics the dining table design.

7

Pawson's distinctive architectural signature avoids doorjambs and frames; wherever possible his doors are full length, floor to ceiling. The door off the entrance corridor is identical to the closet doors that continue along the walls.

8

Constructed on site from the same massive planks that were used for the floor, these stools reinforce the majesty of simplicity. Patience, time and opportunity have conspired to create memorable and monumental pieces of furniture.

OPPOSITE PAGE

There is a mathematical precision to Pawson's pared-down approach. The tall, elegant front door fills the entire entrance space and its width is twice that of the floorboards of the corridor.

Pawson's approach is not limited to smallish urban spaces. Mount Eagle, the home of clients in Ireland idyllically situated overlooking the sea, has benefited equally from his creative imprint.

Connoisseurs of Georgian architecture will tell you that the best work is in Ireland. In London, brickwork was stuccoed to look like stone; in Ireland, they built in real stone. A more sober character, no doubt influenced by budget restrictions, reduced the external decoration to an absolute minimum. Thus the pared-down classicism that was the ideal of Georgian London found its most perfect expression in Ireland.

Mount Eagle is a Georgian house of undisputed distinction into which Pawson has introduced his own signature elements. The result is one of pure harmony. The strong simplicity of his work is reinforced by the classical proportions of the Georgian architecture and large open areas defined by subtle, gently contrasting materials. White plaster walls, French limestone floors and Japanese oak staircases conspire to create an elegantly minimal environment. One can imagine that a hundred years from now this house and its new interior will be listed as a heritage site, so well do the original architecture and the new interior architecture meld.

It also makes a convincing argument for the point central to this book – that the minimalism being practised in London today has its roots in a 'reductivist tradition'. Mount Eagle brings this tradition full circle; past and present unite in a single statement of reduction and refinement.

"There can be no real beauty without singularity of proportion."

Edgar Allan Poe

OPPOSITE PAGE
The grand staircase of this late Georgian house is enhanced by the total lack of clutter and knick-knacks. The ideal of the Georgian model was a return to the pure proportions, shapes and forms of Roman and Greek classicism, and thanks to Pawson's redesign of this interior one suspects that it is now probably closer to the original intention than it has ever been. French limestone floors provide a subtle and pleasing complement to the beautifully crafted Japanese oak stairs.

FOLLOWING PAGES (142–143)
Light from the bay windows illuminates the pristine space; a perfect foil for a pair of Jean Dunand Art Deco chairs, a Baselitz painting, an original white marble fireplace surround and a French stone floor.

MAPPLETHORPE

1	2	3	4	5	6
7	8	9	10	11	12
13	14	15	16	17	18

PHOTOS IN ORDER OF APPEARANCE – PREVIOUS PAGES (144–145)

1

Japanese oak is used for the floors and also to clad this cast iron bath. The entire suite is reduced to two ingredients – white-painted plaster and blond oak.

2 & 14

A 'maquette' of the house sits on one of the original fireplace surrounds. Another fireplace by contrast was newly designed by Pawson.

3

Two chairs designed by Donald Judd, the late great minimal artist, flank a table also of his design.

4

The few pieces of furniture allowed into these pristine spaces are all of exceptional pedigree, in this case an armless chair by French Futurist Jean Prouvé.

5 & 10

Adjoining the house in what once were the stables, Pawson created a genuine gallery to show off modern works such as this painting by Baselitz.

6

A lamp designed by Philippe Starck sits atop the cleverly designed bedhead that slides open to reveal storage space.

7, 9, 12

Oversize French limestone floors feature throughout the house in combination with Japanese oak.

8 & 13

Using the natural beauty of Japanese oak, Pawson has created staircases that are so sculptural and refined that they also function as furniture.

11, 15, 18

Throughout the house, the unadorned simple structures sit comfortably in the massive spaces of the Georgian estate.

16

Apart from furniture by Donald Judd and Jean Prouvé, the collection is rounded out by very beautiful examples of Jean Dunand's Art Deco designs.

17

Pawson's staircases appear to float from the wall because the timber treads finish short of the wall.

OPPOSITE PAGE

Three rooms were knocked together to create a single bedroom and bathroom suite, a free-flowing space dissected by a green frosted glass wall.

MR

MINIMUM

CLAUDIO SILVESTRIN

In discussing the work of architect Claudio Silvestrin, and in particular the philosophy that drives his work, it is impossible not to repeat most of what has been said about Pawson.

Silvestrin and Pawson are architectural soulmates. Their work is on the same spiritual plane; they share the same values.

Claudio Silvestrin is motivated by reduction. His is a monastic architecture that seeks beauty through emptiness, a sophisticated use of simplicity to achieve spaces of a very different kind of monumentality. He wants to do away with useless decoration and instead fill space with what Juliette Malagodi refers to as 'vibrant spirituality'.

It is not surprising, then, that he and Pawson were once partners. In fact, so intertwined has their input been on previous joint projects and so alike are their 'manifestos' that it is virtually impossible to extract from their joint projects what came from whom and when. As two highly creative individuals, they probably had too much drive, dedication and conviction to stand much chance of staying together for very long. While they were together, however, they did work on a host of exceptional projects.

Silvestrin is originally Italian and his work, in its impressive and faultlessly executed detailing (the true strength and foundation of his approach), leans towards a more Mediterranean palette of materials. He works with Siena stone (Tuscan *pietra serena*) and Burgundy Beauval stone, picks out Gio Ponti's elegant Superleggera chair for particular attention and, interestingly, works mostly in the south, in Provence and on Mallorca. It is as if Silvestrin and his old partner had decided on a line of demarcation: 'I get the south, you get the north.' There is, without doubt, intense rivalry between the two. It is almost as if they were involved in a competition to out-'minimalize' each other. The clear winners in this game of design one-upmanship are the clients.

It would be fair to say that Silvestrin is more the 'artist' of the two. He seems least inclined to compromise and has applied his code to each and every facet of his private life: his clothes, food, coffee, even his haircut (or perhaps it's just because